Keto Sea

MW00800378

Easy And Delicious Low Carb And High Fat Recipes - Only Fish Dishes

Sandy Lewis

TABLE OF CONTENTS

Buttery and Seasoned Shrimps

Preparation time: 5 minutes Cooking

Time: 6 minutes Servings: 4

INGREDIENTS

- 1½lb jumbo shrimps, peeled and deveined
- Salt and freshly cracked black pepper to taste
- ½ tsp paprika
- 1 tsp Old Bay seasoning
- 1 tsp Worcestershire sauce
- 1 tbsp unsalted butter
- ½ tbsp lemon juice
- 1/4 cup yogurt

INSTRUCTIONS:

1. Switch on the instant pot, insert the inner pot, add shrimps in it along with remaining Ingredients, stir well, and shut with the lid.

2. Press the 'manual' button, cook the shrimps for 6 minutes at high pressure, and when the timer beeps, do quick pressure release.

3. For meal prep, let shrimps cool completely, then distribute between four air-tight containers, add cooked noodles or rice in it and store in the refrigerator for up to two days.

4. When ready to eat, reheat shrimps in the microwave until hot and then serve.

NUTRITION: Calories 189, Total Fat 6.6g, Total Carbs 6.5g, Protein 24.1, Sugar 0g, Fiber 3.2g, Sodium 431mg

Healthy Halibut Soup with Ginger

Preparation time: 5 minutes Cooking Time:

35 minutes Servings: 6

GREDIENTS

- 1 tbsp olive oil
- 1 large white onion, peeled, chopped
- 2 tbsp fresh ginger, peeled, minced
- 2 cups chicken broth
- 1 cup of water
- 1lb halibut, cut into 1-inch pieces
- Sea salt, to taste
- ½ tsp cracked black pepper

TRUCTIONS:

1. Take a large pot, place it over medium heat, add oil and when hot, add onions and cook for 8 minutes or until sauté.
2. Then add ginger to chicken broth and water, stir and bring the mixture to boil.
3. Switch heat to the low level, simmer the soup for 20 minutes until vegetables are tender, then remove the pot from heat and puree the soup with an immersion blender until smooth.

4. Return pot over medium heat, add halibut into the soup, season with salt and black pepper, stir and simmer the soup for 5 minutes until hot.

5. Ladle soup into bowls and serve.

NUTRITION: Calories 246, Total Fat 16.3g, Total Carbs 8g, Protein 16.3g, Sugar 3.4g, Sodium 363mg

Shrimp and Mushroom Soup with Cheddar

Preparation time: 5 minutes Cooking

Time: 18 minutes Servings: 8

INGREDIENTS

- 32oz chicken broth
- 8oz shredded cheddar cheese
- 1 cup heavy whipping cream
- ½ cup unsalted butter
- 24oz   shrimp,   extra-small,   peeled, deveined
- 2 cups mushrooms, sliced

STRUCTIONS:

1. Take a large pot, place it over medium heat, pour in the broth, and bring it to a boil.
2. Switch heat to the low level, add cheese, cream, and butter and stir well until combined.
3. Then add shrimps and mushrooms, continue simmering the soup for 15 minutes until shrimps are cooked.

4. Ladle soup into bowls and serve.

NUTRITION: Calories 395, Total Fat 28.7g, Total Carbs 3.3g, Protein 29.8g, Sugar 0.8g, Sodium 1428mg

Creamy Salmon and Leek Soup

Preparation time: 10 minutes Cooking

Time: 35 minutes Servings: 4

INGREDIENTS

- 2 tbsp unsalted butter
- 2 leeks, washed, trimmed and sliced
- 3 garlic cloves, minced
- 6 cups seafood broth
- 2 tsp dried thyme
- Salt and freshly cracked black pepper, to taste
- 1lb salmon, in bite-size pieces
- 1½ cups coconut milk, unsweetened

INSTRUCTIONS:

1. Take a large saucepan, place it over low- medium heat, add butter and when it melts, add leeks and garlic, stir and cook for 3 minutes.

2. Pour in seafood broth, add thyme and simmer the soup for 15 minutes.

3. Then season soup with salt and black pepper, add salmon, pour in milk, and continue simmering for 5 minutes.
4. Ladle soup into bowls and serve.
5. Dish out and serve immediately.

NUTRITION: Calories 332, Total Fat 24.3g, Total Carbs 9.1g, Protein 21.5g, Sugar 3.9g, Sodium 839mg,

Quick Red Shrimps Curry

Preparation time: 5 minutes Cooking
Time: 9 minutes Servings: 4

INGREDIENTS

- 1 tbsp olive oil
- 1 medium onion, peeled, diced
- 1 tbsp minced garlic
- 1 tbsp red curry powder
- 1lb jumbo shrimps, peeled and deveined
- 1 medium green bell pepper, diced
- 1 tsp turmeric
- 1 tsp smoked paprika
- ½ cup garam masala
- 1/4 cup coconut milk, unsweetened

INSTRUCTIONS

1. Switch on the instant pot, insert inner pot, press the 'sauté' button, add oil and when hot, add onion and garlic, season with red curry powder and cook for 3 minutes until fragrant.
2. Then add remaining Ingredients, stir well, shut the instant pot with lid, press the 'manual' button, and

cook at the high- pressure setting for 6 minutes.

3. When instant pot beep, release pressure naturally, open the lid, transfer the curry to a serving dish, and then serve.

4. For meal prep, let curry cool completely, distribute it between four air-tight containers, garnish with cilantro, and store in the refrigerator for up to three days.

5. When ready to eat, reheat curry in the microwave until hot and then serve.

NUTRITION: Calories 165, Total Fat 7.7g, Total Carbs 10.2g, Protein 6.3g, Sugar 2.1g, Fiber 4.2g, Sodium 9mg,

Buttery Salmon Fillets with Asparagus

Preparation time: 5 minutes Cooking

Time: 20 minutes Servings: 2

INGREDIENTS

- 4 stalks of asparagus
- 2 fillets of salmon
- Salt and freshly cracked black pepper, to taste
- ¼ cup unsalted butter
- ¼ cup champagne
- 1 tsp olive oil

INSTRUCTIONS

1. Switch on the oven, then set its temperature to 355°F and let it preheat.

2. Meanwhile, take a bowl, place all the Ingredients in it, and stir until mixed.

3. Take a baking dish, grease it with oil, place prepared mixture in it and then bake for about 20 minutes until thoroughly cooked.

4. When done, remove the baking dish from the oven and let cool completely.

5. For meal prep, distribute salmon and asparagus evenly between two air-tight containers and store in the refrigerator

for up to one day.

6. When ready to eat, reheat salmon and asparagus in the microwave until hot and then serve.

NUTRITION: Calories 475, Total Fat 36.8g, Total Carbs 1.1g, Protein 35.2g, Sugar 0.5g, Sodium 242mg

Buttery Prawns with Lemongrass

Preparation time: 2 hours and 5 minutes

Cooking Time: 15 minutes

Servings: 2

INGREDIENTS

- ½lb prawns, deveined, peeled
- ¼ tsp smoked paprika
- ½ red chili pepper, seeded and chopped
- 6 tbsp unsalted butter
- 2 lemongrass stalks
- 1 tbsp olive oil

INSTRUCTIONS

1. Switch on the oven, then set its temperature to 390°F and let it preheat.

2. Place prawns in a bowl, add paprika, red chili pepper, and butter, toss until well mixed, and then marinate in the refrigerator for a minimum of 2 hours.

3. After 2 hours, thread marinated prawns on lemongrass stalks, place them on a baking dish greased with oil and then bake for 15 minutes until prawns have cooked.

4. Serve straight away.

5. For meal prep, let prawns cool completely, then distribute evenly between two air-tight containers and store in the refrigerator for up to four days.

6. When ready to eat, reheat prawns in the microwave until hot and then serve.

NUTRITION: Calories 322, Total Fat 18g, Total Carbs 3.8g, Protein 34.8g, Sugar 0.1g, Sodium 478mg

Buttery and Creamy Shrimp with Paprika

Preparation time: 5 minutes

Cooking Time: 15 minutes Servings: 2

INGREDIENTS

- ½lb shrimp, peeled, deveined
- ¼ tbsp smoked paprika
- Salt and freshly cracked black pepper, to taste
- 1/8 cup unsalted butter
- 1/8 cup sour cream
- 1 tbsp olive oil

INSTRUCTIONS:

1. Switch on the oven, then set its temperature to 390°F and let it preheat.
2. Place shrimps in a bowl, add remaining Ingredients and toss until well coated.
3. Take a baking dish, grease it with oil, then add shrimps in it and bake for 15 minutes until thoroughly cooked.
4. When done, remove the baking dish from the oven and let shrimps cool completely.

5. For meal prep, let shrimps cool completely, then distribute evenly between two air-tight containers and store in the refrigerator for up to two days.

6. When ready to eat, reheat shrimps in the microwave until hot and then serve.

Delicious and Simple Salmon Stew

Preparation time: 5 minutes

Cooking Time: 15 minutes Servings: 2

INGREDIENTS

- 1lb salmon fillet, sliced
- Salt, to taste
- ½ tsp red chili powder
- 1 medium white onion, peeled, chopped
- 1 tbsp unsalted butter, melted
- 1 cup fish broth

INSTRUCTIONS:

7. Place salmon fillets in a dish and then season with salt and red chili powder.

8. Take a skillet pan, place it over medium heat, add butter and when it melts, add

   onion and cook for 3 minutes or until saute.

9. Then add salmon, cook for 2 minutes per side, pour in the broth, and cook for 7 minutes until done, covering the pan with lid.

10. Serve straight away.

11. For meal prep, let salmon cool completely, then distribute evenly between two air-tight containers and the store in the refrigerator for up to two days.

12. When ready to eat, reheat salmon in the microwave until hot and then serve.

NUTRITION: Calories 272, Total Fat 14.2g, Total Carbs 4.4g, Protein 32.1g, Sugar 1.9g

Sour and Sweet Fish with Cider and Stevia

Preparation time: 5 minutes

Cooking Time: 15 minutes Servings: 2

INGREDIENTS

- ¼ cup unsalted butter, melted
- 1lb fish chunks
- Salt and freshly cracked black pepper, to taste
- 2 drops of stevia
- 1 tbsp apple cider vinegar

INSTRUCTIONS:

1. Take a skillet pan, place it over medium heat, add butter and when it melts, add fish and cook for 3 minutes.
2. Then season fish with salt and black pepper, add stevia and vinegar, stir until mixed and cook for 10 minutes.
3. Serve straight away.

4. For meal prep, let fish cool completely, then distribute evenly between two air-tight   containers   and store   in   the refrigerator for up to two days.

5. When ready to eat, reheat fish in the microwave until hot and then serve.

NUTRITION: Calories 258, Total Fat 16.7g, Total Carbs 2.8g, Protein 24.5g, Sugar 2.7g, Sodium 649mg

Fancy Salmon and Egg Salad

Preparation time: 3 hours and 5 minutes

Cooking Time: 0 minutes

Servings: 2

INGREDIENTS

- 6oz cooked salmon, chopped
- ½ of medium white onion, peeled, chopped
- 2 stalks of celery, chopped
- 4 organic eggs, hard-boiled, peeled, cubed
- 1 tbsp fresh dill, chopped
- Salt and freshly cracked black pepper, to taste
- ¾ cup avocado mayonnaise

INSTRUCTIONS:

1. Take a large bowl, add salmon in it, then add remaining Ingredients and stir until well combined.
2. Cover the bowl with a plastic wrap and then refrigerate for a minimum of 3 hours before serving.
3. For meal prep, transfer salmon salad into an airtight container and store in the refrigerator for up to 3 days.

4. When ready to eat, reheat salmon in the microwave until hot and then serve.

NUTRITION: Calories 303, Total Fat 30g, Total Carbs 1.7g, Protein 10.3g, Sugar 1g, Sodium 314mg

Omega3 Salmon and Jalapeno Salad

Preparation time: 5 minutes

Cooking Time: 10 minutes

Servings: 2

INGREDIENTS

- ½lb salmon fillet, skinless, cut into 4 steaks
- ¼ tbsp lime juice
- 1 tbsp olive oil, divided
- 4 tbsp sour cream
- ¼ of zucchini, cut into small cubes
- ¼ tsp jalapeño pepper, seeded, chopped
- Salt and freshly cracked black pepper, to taste
- ¼ tbsp fresh dill, chopped

INSTRUCTIONS:

1. Take a skillet pan, place it over medium heat, add oil and when hot, add salmon and cook for 5 minutes per side.

2. Then season salmon with salt and black pepper, stir well, and then transfer to a plate.

3. Place remaining Ingredients in a bowl, stir well, then top it over salmon and serve.

NUTRITION: Calories 291, Total Fat 21.1g, Total Carbs 2.5g, Protein 23.1g, Sugar 0.6g, Sodium 112mg

Roasted Vegetables with Salmon

Preparation time: 15 minutes

Cooking Time: 16 minutes Servings: 3

INGREDIENTS

- 1 cup of water
- 2 cups broccoli florets
- 3 fillets of salmon
- 1 tbsp lemon juice
- 1/4 tsp garlic powder
- Salt and freshly cracked black pepper to taste
- ½ tsp cumin powder
- 1/4 tsp red chili powder
- 1 tbsp olive oil

INSTRUCTIONS:

1. Switch on the instant pot, pour in water, insert a trivet stand, place broccoli on it, and shut with the lid.
2. Press the 'steam' button, cook it for 10 minutes at high-pressure setting, and when instant pot beeps, do quick pressure release.
3. Then open the instant pot, transfer broccoli to a dish and let cool for 10 minutes.
4. Meanwhile, place salmon fillets in a shallow dish, drizzle

with lemon juice, and then sprinkle with garlic, salt, black pepper, cumin, and red chili powder.

5. Drain the instant pot, press the 'sauté' button, grease the inner pot with oil, then add salmon in it and cook for 3 minutes per side until seared.

6. For meal prep, distribute vegetables and salmon between three air-tight containers, and the store in the refrigerator for up to three days.

7. When ready to eat, reheat vegetables and salmon in the microwave until hot and then serve.

NUTRITION: Calories 348, Total Fat 17.5g, Total Carbs 21.2g, Protein 26.5g, Sugar 4.6g, Fiber 10.3g, Sodium 561mg,

Scallops Pasta with Vermicelli

Preparation time: 10 minutes

Cooking Time: 7 minutes

Servings: 4

INGREDIENTS

- 1 tsp olive oil
- 1 tsp unsalted butter
- 1 tsp minced garlic
- 3/4lb sea scallops
- Salt and freshly cracked black pepper to taste
- ½ cup dry vermouth wine
- 2 cups vermicelli noodles, cooked
- 1 tbsp fresh basil, chopped

INSTRUCTIONS:

1. Switch on the instant pot, insert the inner pot, press the sauté button, add oil and butter and when the butter melts, add garlic and cook for 1 minute until

fragrant.

2. Add scallops, stir well, season with salt and black pepper, then pour in the wine, and shut with the lid.

3. Press the 'manual' button, cook for 6 minutes at pressure setting, and when instant pot beeps release pressure naturally.

4. For meal prep, distribute vermicelli noodles between four air-tight containers, top with scallops, then garnish with basil and refrigerate for up to three days.

5. When ready to eat, reheat scallops in the microwave until hot and then serve.

NUTRITION: Calories389, Total Carbs 25g, Protein 35.5g, Total Fat 6.5g, Sugar 0, Fiber 13.8g, Sodium 678,

Delicious Scallops with Roasted Bell Pepper

Preparation time: 5 minutes

Cooking Time: 11 minutes

Servings: 4

INGREDIENTS

- 30 scallops
- 2 red bell peppers, deseeded, julienned
- 1½ tsp dried oregano
- ½ cup dry white wine
- 1 cup chicken broth
- 1 tbsp unsalted butter, chilled
- 1 tbsp cornstarch
- 3 tbsp water
- 1 tbsp chopped fresh basil

INSTRUCTIONS:

1. Switch on the instant pot, add scallops and bell pepper in it, sprinkle with oregano, drizzle with wine, pour in the broth, stir well, and shut with the lid.

2. Press the 'manual' button, cook for 6 minutes at a high heat setting, and when the timer beeps, do quick pressure release.

3. Then open the instant pot, press the

'sauté' button and add butter in it.

4. Stir together cornstarch and water, add into the instant pot, stir until mixed and simmer for 3 to 5 minutes until the sauce has thickened to the desired level.

5. For meal prep, distribute scallops between four air-tight containers, add some cooked rice, then garnish with basil and refrigerate for up to three days.

6. When ready to eat, reheat scallops in the microwave until hot and then serve.

NUTRITION: Calories 357, Total Carbs11.9 g, Protein 43.8g, Total Fat 14.1g, Sugar 0.9g, Fiber 4.2g, Sodium 550mg,

Filling Taco Meal with Shrimp

Preparation time: 5 minutes

Cooking Time: 6 minutes Servings: 4

INGREDIENTS

- 1 tbsp olive oil
- ½ tsp minced garlic
- 20 medium shrimps, peeled and deveined
- Salt and freshly cracked black pepper to taste
- ½ tsp red chili powder
- ½ tsp ground cumin
- 1 cup tomatoes, diced
- ½ cup shredded cheddar cheese, grated
- 1 lime, cut into 4 slices

INSTRUCTIONS:

1. Switch on the instant pot, press the 'sauté' button, add oil in the inner pot, add garlic and cook for 1 minute until fragrant.

2. Add shrimps, season with salt, black pepper, red chili powder, and cumin, stir well, cook for 5 minutes until shrimps turn pink, then transfer shrimps to a dish and let cool completely.

3. For meal prep, distribute tomatoes in an air-tight

containers, add shrimps, garnish with cheese and lime wedges and refrigerate for up to three days.

4. When ready to eat, reheat shrimp taco meal in the microwave until hot and then serve.

NUTRITION: Calories 605, Total Fat 7.8g, Total Carbs 112.2g, Protein 23.6g, Sugar 10.3g, Fiber 43.9g, Sodium 268mg,

Simple and Flavorful Swordfish Mexicana

Preparation time: 5 minutes

Cooking Time: 10 minutes

Servings: 2

INGREDIENTS

- 2 steaks of Swordfish
    - 1 cup tomato
    - 1½ tbsp lime juice, freshly squeezed
    - 1/8 tsp ground cumin
    - 1/4 cup water
    - ½ tsp minced garlic
    - Salt and freshly cracked black pepper to taste

INSTRUCTIONS:

1. Switch on the instant pot, add swordfish steaks in the inner pot, then add remaining Ingredients, stir until just mixed and shut with the lid.

2. Press the manual button, cook for 10 minutes at a high-pressure setting, and when the timer beeps, do natural pressure release.

3. Open the lid, let fish cool completely, distribute it between two air-tight meal prep containers, add some

cooked rice and refrigerate for up to three days.

4. When ready to eat, reheat fish in the microwave until hot and then serve.

NUTRITION: Calories 522, Total Fat 32.9g, Total Carbs 6.5g, Protein 47.6g, Sugar 1.2g, Fiber 3.4g, Sodium 839mg,

Avocado and Herring Fat Bombs

Preparation Time: 5 minutes Servings 4

NUTRITION: 316 Calories; 24.4g Fat; 5.9g Carbs; 17.4g
Protein; 4.2g Fiber

INGREDIENTS

- 1 avocado, pitted and peeled
- 1/2 cup scallions, chopped
- 1 teaspoon capers
- 1 can herring
- Salt and black pepper, to taste
- 3 ounces sunflower seeds
- 1/2 teaspoon hot paprika

DIRECTIONS

1. In a mixing bowl, combine all Ingredients until well
   incorporated. Roll the mixture into 8 balls.
2. Storing

3. Place the fat bombs in airtight containers or Ziploc bags; keep in your refrigerator for up to 3 to 4 days.

4. To freeze, arrange the fat bombs on a baking tray in a single layer; freeze for about 2 hours. Transfer the frozen bombs to an airtight container. Freeze for up to 2 months. Bon appétit!

Saucy Tuna with Brussels Sprouts

Preparation Time: 25 minutes Servings 4

NUTRITION: 372 Calories; 27.8g Fat; 5.6g Carbs; 26.5g Protein; 2.2g Fiber

INGREDIENTS

- 1 pound tuna
- 1 tablespoon fresh lemon juice
- 1/4 cup extra-virgin olive oil
- 1 tomato, chopped
- Sea salt and freshly ground black pepper, to taste
- 1 teaspoon dried rosemary
- 1/2 cup fish stock
- 1/2 pounds Brussels sprouts
- 1/4 cup parsley
- 2 garlic cloves, crushed
- 1/3 cup pine nuts, chopped

DIRECTIONS

1. Brush a non-stick skillet with cooking spray. Once hot, cook the tuna steaks for about 4 minutes per side; sprinkle with

salt, pepper, and rosemary; set aside.

2. In the same skillet, cook Brussels sprouts; adding the fish stock to prevent over cooking. Then, sauté for about 5 minutes

   or until the Brussels sprouts are crisp- tender.

3. Add in the chopped tomatoes and continue to cook for 3 minutes more. Fold in the reserved tuna steaks.

4. Process the parsley, garlic, pine nuts, lemon juice, and olive oil in your food processor or blender until it reaches a paste consistency. Reserve.

5. Storing

6. Place the tuna steaks in airtight containers and keep in your refrigerator for up to 3 to 4 days.

7. Place the sauce in airtight containers and keep in your refrigerator for up to 3 to 4 days.

8. For freezing, place the tuna steaks in airtight containers or wrap tightly with freezer wrap. Freeze up to 2 to 3 months. Defrost in the refrigerator.

9. Top with the sauce and serve. Bon appétit!

Greek Salad with Grilled Halloumi

Preparation Time: 15 minutes

Servings 4

NUTRITION: 199 Calories; 10.6g Fat; 6.1g Carbs; 14.2g Protein; 1.1g Fiber

INGREDIENTS

- 1 pound halibut steak
- 1 cup cherry tomatoes, halved
- 1 onion, thinly sliced
- 1 tablespoon lemon juice
- 1 Lebanese cucumbers, thinly sliced
- 1/2 cup radishes, thinly sliced
- 2 tablespoons sunflower seeds
- 1 ½ tablespoons extra-virgin olive oil
- 1/2 head butterhead lettuce
- 1 cup Halloumi cheese
- Sea salt and pepper, to taste

DIRECTIONS

1. Cook the halibut steak on preheated grill for 5 to 6 minutes per side. until the fish flakes easily with a fork.

2. Grill the halloumi cheese and slice into small pieces.

3. Toss the grilled halloumi cheese with the remaining Ingredients and set aside.

4. Storing

5. Divide the halibut steaks between airtight containers; keep in your refrigerator for up to 3 to 4 days.

6. Place the Greek salad in airtight containers or Ziploc bags; keep in your refrigerator for up to 3 to 4 days.

7. For freezing, place the halibut steaks in airtight containers or wrap tightly with freezer wrap. Freeze up to 2 to 3 months. Defrost in the refrigerator.

8. Serve with chilled salad and enjoy!

Italian-Style Seafood Stew

Preparation Time: 20 minutes Servings 4

NUTRITION: 209 Calories; 12.6g Fat; 6.6g Carbs; 15.2g Protein; 2g Fiber

INGREDIENTS

- 2 tablespoons lard, room temperature
- 1/2 teaspoon lime zest
- 1/2 pound shrimp
- 1/2 pound scallops
- 1 teaspoon Italian seasonings blend
- Salt and ground black pepper, to taste
- 1 leek, chopped
- 2 garlic cloves, pressed
- 1 cup tomato puree
- 1 celery stalk, chopped
- 3 cups fish stock
- 2 tablespoons port wine

DIRECTIONS

9. Melt the lard in a large pot over a moderately high heat. Sauté the leek and garlic until they've softened.

10. Stir in the pureed tomatoes and continue to cook for about 10 minutes.

11. Add in the remaining Ingredients and bring to a boil. Turn the heat to a simmer and continue to cook for 4 to 5 minutes.

12. Storing

13. Spoon your stew into airtight containers; keep in your refrigerator for up 3 to 4 days.

14. For freezing, spoon your stew into airtight containers or heavy-duty freezer bags. Freeze up to 4 to 6 months. Defrost in the microwave or refrigerator. Enjoy!

Creole Tuna with Lemon

Preparation Time: 40 minutes

Servings 4

NUTRITION: 266 Calories; 11.5g Fat; 5.6g Carbs; 34.9g Protein; 0.7g Fiber

INGREDIENTS

- 4 tuna fillets
- 1/4 cup scallions, chopped
- 2 garlic cloves, minced
- 1/3 cup fresh lemon juice
- 1/3 cup coconut aminos
- 3 teaspoons olive oil
- 1 teaspoon lemon thyme
- Salt and ground black pepper
- 1 teaspoon dried rosemary

DIRECTIONS

1. Place all Nutritional Info per Serving: in a ceramic dish; cover and let it marinate for about 30 minutes in the refrigerator.

2. Grill the tuna fillets for about 15 minutes, basting with the reserved marinade.

3. Storing

4. Place the tuna steaks in airtight containers and keep in your refrigerator for up to 3 to 4 days.

5. For freezing, place the tuna steaks in airtight containers or wrap tightly with freezer wrap. Freeze up to 2 to 3 months. Defrost in the refrigerator.

Pan-Seared Halibut with Herb Sauce

Preparation Time: 20 minutes Servings 4

NUTRITION: 273 Calories; 19.2g Fat; 4.3g Carbs; 22.6g Protein; 0.7g Fiber

INGREDIENTS

- 2 tablespoons butter, at room temperature
- 4 halibut steaks
- 1 teaspoon garlic
- 1 ½ tablespoons extra-virgin olive oil
- 1/2 cup white onions, chopped
- 1 tablespoon fish sauce
- Salt and ground black pepper, to taste
- 1 tablespoon soy sauce
- 2 cloves garlic, finely minced
- 3 tablespoons fish consommé
- 2 tablespoons fresh coriander, chopped
- 1/4 cup Italian parsley, finely chopped
- 1 tablespoon fresh lemon juice

DIRECTIONS

6. Melt the butter in a saucepan over medium-high heat.

7. Once hot, sear the halibut for 6 to 7 minutes until cooked all the way through. Reserve.

8. In the same pan, sauté the onions and garlic until tender and fragrant. Add in the fish consommé along with the coriander, fish sauce, and reserved halibut steaks; continue to cook, partially covered, for 5 to 6 minutes.

9. Whisk the remaining Ingredients for the herb sauce.

10. Storing

11. Place the pan-sear halibut in airtight containers and keep in your refrigerator for up to 3 to 4 days.

12. Place the herb sauce in airtight containers and keep in your refrigerator for up to 3 to 4 days.

13. For freezing, place the pan-sear halibut in airtight containers or wrap tightly with freezer wrap. Freeze up to 2 to 3 months. Defrost in the refrigerator.

Pepper Boats with Herring

Preparation Time: 10 minutes Servings 4

NUTRITION: 120 Calories; 5.4g Fat; 5.8g Carbs; 12.3g Protein; 1.6g Fiber

INGREDIENTS

- 4 pickled peppers, slice into halves
- 8 ounces canned herring, drained
- 1 teaspoon Dijon mustard
- 1 celery, chopped
- 1 cup onions, chopped
- Salt and freshly ground black pepper, to taste
- 1 tablespoon fresh coriander, chopped

DIRECTIONS

1. Broil the bell pepper for 5 to 6 minutes until they've softened. Cut into halves and discard the seeds.

2. In a mixing bowl, thoroughly combine the herring, Dijon mustard, celery, onions, salt, black pepper, and fresh coriander.

3. Mix to combine well. Spoon the mixture into the bell pepper halves.

4. Storing

5. Place the stuffed peppers in airtight containers; keep in your refrigerator for 3 to 4 days.

6. Wrap each stuffed pepper tightly in several layers of plastic wrap and squeeze the air out. Place them in airtight containers; they can be frozen for up to 1 month.

7. Reheat the thawed peppers at 200 degrees F until they are completely warm. Enjoy!

Oven-Baked Sole Fillets

Preparation Time: 30 minutes Servings 4

NUTRITION: 195 Calories; 8.2g Fat; 0.5g Carbs; 28.7g Protein; 0.6g Fiber

INGREDIENTS

- 2 tablespoons olive oil
- 1/2 tablespoon Dijon mustard
- 1 teaspoon garlic paste
- 1/2 tablespoon fresh ginger, minced
- 1/2 teaspoon porcini powder
- Salt and ground black pepper, to taste
- 1/2 teaspoon paprika
- 4 sole fillets
- 1/4 cup fresh parsley, chopped

DIRECTIONS

1. Combine the oil, Dijon mustard, garlic paste, ginger, porcini powder, salt, black pepper and paprika.

2. Rub this mixture all over sole fillets. Place the sole fillets in a lightly oiled baking pan.

3. Bake in the preheated oven at 400 degrees F for about 20 minutes.

4. Storing

5. Place the sole fillets in airtight containers and keep in your refrigerator for up to 3 to 4 days.

6. For freezing, place the sole fillets in airtight containers or wrap tightly with freezer wrap. Freeze up to 2 to 3 months. Defrost in the refrigerator. Serve with fresh parsley.

Old-Fashioned Seafood Chowder

Preparation Time: 15 minutes Servings

5

NUTRITION: 404 Calories; 30g Fat; 5.3g Carbs; 23.9g Protein; 0.3g Fiber

INGREDIENTS

- 1/2 stick butter
- 3/4 pound prawns, peeled and deveined
- 1/2 pound crab meat
- 2 tablespoons scallions, chopped
- 1 tablespoon tomato sauce
- 1 teaspoon Mediterranean spice mix
- 1 egg, lightly beaten
- 2 garlic cloves, minced
- 1/3 cup port wine
- 1 quart chicken bone broth
- 2 cups double cream

DIRECTIONS

1. In a heavy bottomed pot, melt the butter over a moderately high flame. Sauté the scallions and garlic

until they've softened.

2. Add in the prawns, crab meat, wine, and chicken bone broth. Continue to cook until thoroughly heated for 5 to 6 minutes.

3. Decrease the heat to low; add in the remaining Ingredients and continue to simmer for 5 minutes more.

4. Storing

5. Spoon your chowder into airtight containers; keep in your refrigerator for up 3 to 4 days.

6. For freezing, spoon your chowder into airtight containers or heavy-duty freezer bags. Freeze up to 4 to 6 months. Defrost in the microwave or refrigerator. Enjoy!

Green Salad with Crab Mayo

Preparation Time: 15 minutes Servings 4

NUTRITION: 293 Calories; 27.1g Fat; 6.3g Carbs; 9.3g Protein; 3.3g Fiber

INGREDIENTS

For the Crab Mayo:

- 1 pound crabmeat
- 2 egg yolks
- Coarse sea salt and ground black pepper, to season
- 1 teaspoon garlic, pressed
- 1/2 teaspoon basil
- 1/2 tablespoon Dijon mustard
- 3/4 cup extra-virgin olive oil
- 1/2 teaspoon Sriracha sauce
- 2 tablespoons fresh lime juice

For the Salad:

- A bunch of scallions, chopped
- 1 cup radishes, sliced
- 1 head Romaine lettuce

- 1 cup Arugula
- 1 Spanish pepper, julienned

DIRECTIONS

1. Mix the egg yolks and mustard in your blender; pour in the oil in a tiny stream, and continue to blend.
2. Now, add in the Sriracha sauce, lime juice, salt, black pepper, garlic, basil, and crabmeat.
3. Toss the remaining Ingredients in a salad bowl. Add in prepared crab mayo sauce and gently stir to combine.
4. Storing
5. Place your salad in airtight containers and keep in your refrigerator for up to 3 to 4 days. Serve well-chilled.

Parmesan Crusted Cod

Preparation Time: 15 minutes Servings 4

NUTRITION: 222 Calories; 12.6g Fat; 0.9g Carbs; 27.9g
Protein; 0.3g Fiber

INGREDIENTS

- 1 pound cod fillets, cut into 4 servings
- 2 tablespoons olive oil
- 1/2 teaspoon paprika
- 3/4 cup grated Parmesan cheese
- Flaky sea salt and ground black pepper, to taste

DIRECTIONS

1. In a shallow mixing dish, combine the salt pepper, paprika, and Parmesan cheese,
2. Press the cod fillets into this Parmesan mixture.
3. Heat the olive oil in a nonstick skillet over medium-high flame. Cook the cod fillets for 12 to 15 minutes or until opaque.
4. Storing
5. Place the Parmesan crusted cod in airtight containers and keep in your refrigerator for up to 3 to 4 days.

6. For freezing, place the Parmesan crusted cod in airtight containers or wrap tightly with freezer wrap. Freeze up to 2 to 3 months. Defrost in the refrigerator. Bon appétit!

Colorful Prawn Salad

Preparation Time: 10 minutes + chilling time Servings 6

NUTRITION: 209 Calories; 9.5g Fat; 6.8g Carbs; 20.2g Protein; 0.4g Fiber

INGREDIENTS

- 1 medium-sized lemon, cut into wedges
- 2 pounds prawns
- 1/2 cup mayonnaise
- 1/2 cup cream cheese
- 1/2 teaspoon stone-ground mustard
- 1 tablespoon dry sherry
- 1 tablespoon balsamic vinegar
- Salt and black pepper
- 4 scallion stalks, chopped
- 1 Italian pepper, sliced
- 1 cucumber, sliced
- 1 ½ cups radishes, sliced
- 1 tablespoon Sriracha sauce

DIRECTIONS

1. Bring a pot of a lightly salted water to a boil over high heat. Add in the lemon and prawns and cook approximately 3 minutes, until they are opaque. Drain and rinse your prawns.

2. In a salad bowl, toss the remaining Ingredients until well combined.

3. Storing

4. Place the cooked prawns in airtight containers or Ziploc bags; keep in your refrigerator for up 3 to 4 days.

5. For freezing, arrange the cooked prawns in a single layer on a baking tray; place in

   the freezer for about 15 minutes, or until it begins to harden.

6. Transfer the frozen prawns to heavy-duty freezer bags. Freeze up to 3 months. Defrost in your refrigerator.

7. Place the salad in airtight containers or Ziploc bags; keep in your refrigerator for up 3 to 4 days. Top with the prepared prawns and serve!

Classic Tuna and Avocado Salad

Preparation Time: 20 minutes Servings 4

NUTRITION: 244 Calories; 12.7g Fat; 5.3g Carbs; 23.4g Protein; 4.4g Fiber

INGREDIENTS

- 1 ½ pounds tuna steaks
- 1 avocado, pitted, peeled and diced
- Salt and ground black pepper, to taste
- 2 tablespoons fresh lemon juice
- 1 head lettuce
- 1/2 cup black olives, pitted and sliced
- 2 Italian peppers, deveined and sliced
- 1 cup grape tomatoes, halved
- 1 shallot, chopped
- 1/4 cup mayonnaise

DIRECTIONS

1. Grill the tuna steaks for about 15 minutes; cut into chunks.
2. In a salad bowl, mix lettuce, peppers, tomatoes, shallot, and avocado.

3. Then, make the dressing by mixing the mayonnaise, salt, pepper and lime juice. Dress the salad and toss to combine. Top with black olives.

4. Storing

5. Place the tuna steaks in airtight containers and keep in your refrigerator for up to 3 to 4 days.

6. Place the salad in airtight containers and keep in your refrigerator for up to 3 to 4 days.

7. For freezing, place the tuna steaks in airtight containers or wrap tightly with freezer wrap. Freeze up to 2 to 3 months. Defrost in the refrigerator.

8. Top your salad with the tuna chunks and serve!

Salmon and Ricotta Stuffed Tomatoes

Preparation Time: 30 minutes Servings 6

NUTRITION: 303 Calories; 22.9g Fat; 6.8g Carbs; 17g Protein; 1.6g Fiber

INGREDIENTS

- 6 tomatoes, pulp and seeds removed
- 1 ½ cups Ricotta cheese
- 10 ounces salmon
- 1 cup scallions, finely chopped
- 2 garlic cloves, minced
- 2 tablespoons coriander, chopped
- 1/2 cup aioli
- 1 teaspoon Dijon mustard
- Sea salt and ground black pepper, to taste

DIRECTIONS

1. Grill your salmon for about 10 minutes until browned and flakes easily with a fork. Cut into small chunks.
2. Thoroughly combine the salmon, scallions, garlic, coriander, aioli, mustard, salt, and pepper in a bowl.

3. Spoon the filling into tomatoes. Bake in the preheated oven at 390 degrees F for

   17 to 20 minutes until they are thoroughly cooked.

4. Storing

6. Place the stuffed tomatoes in airtight containers; keep in your refrigerator for 3 Wrap each stuffed tomato tightly in several layers of plastic wrap and squeeze the air out. Place them in airtight containers; they can be frozen for up to 1 month.

7. Reheat the thawed stuffed tomatoes at 200 degrees F until they are completely warm. Top with the Ricotta cheese and place under preheated broiled for 5 minutes until hot and bubbly. Enjoy!

Seafood Gumbo with a Twist

Preparation Time: 25 minutes Servings 4

NUTRITION: 481 Calories; 26.9g Fat; 5g Carbs; 46.6g Protein; 1.3g Fiber

INGREDIENTS

- 2 tablespoons lard, melted
- 2 breakfast sausages, cut crosswise into 1/2-inch-thick slices
- 2 garlic cloves, finely minced
- 1 yellow onion, chopped
- 1 cup tomatoes, pureed
- 1 tablespoon fish sauce
- 3/4 cup fish consommé
- 1/3 cup port wine
- 1/2 pound tilapia, cut into chunks
- 20 sea scallops
- 2 tablespoons fresh coriander, chopped

DIRECTIONS

1. In a stock pot, melt the lard over medium-high heat. Cook the sausages for about 5 minutes until no longer pink; reserve.

2. Now, sauté the onion and garlic until they've softened; reserve.

3. Add in the pureed tomatoes, fish sauce, fish consommé and wine; let it simmer for another 15 minutes.

4. Add in the tilapia, scallops, coriander, and reserved sausages. Continue to simmer, partially covered, for 5 to 6 minutes.

5. Storing

6. Spoon your gumbo into airtight containers; keep in your refrigerator for up 3 to 4 days.

7. For freezing, spoon your gumbo into airtight containers or heavy-duty freezer bags. Freeze up to 4 to 6 months. Defrost in the microwave or refrigerator. Garnish with coriander and enjoy!

Haddock and Vegetable Skewers

Preparation Time: 15 minutes Servings 4

NUTRITION: 257 Calories; 12.5g Fat; 7g Carbs; 27.5g Protein; 0.9g Fiber

INGREDIENTS

- 1 pound haddock, cut into small cubes
- Salt and pepper, to taste
- 1/2 teaspoon basil
- 2 tablespoons olive oil
- 1 red onion, cut into wedges
- 1 zucchini, diced
- 1 cup cherry tomatoes
- 2 tablespoons coconut aminos

DIRECTIONS

1. Start by preheating your grill on high.
2. Toss the haddock and vegetables with salt, pepper, basil, olive oil, and coconut aminos.
3. Alternate the seasoned haddock, onion, zucchini and tomatoes on bamboo skewers.

4. Grill your skewers for 5 minutes for medium-rare, flipping them occasionally to ensure even cooking.

5. Storing

6. Divide the grilled skewers between four airtight containers; keep in your refrigerator for up to 3 to 4 days.

7. For freezing, place the grilled skewers in airtight containers or wrap tightly with freezer wrap. Freeze up to 2 to 3 months. Defrost in the refrigerator. Bon appétit!

. Avocado and Shrimp Salad

Preparation Time: 10 minutes + chilling time Servings 6

NUTRITION: 236 Calories; 14.3g Fat; 5.3g Carbs; 16.3g Protein; 3g Fiber

INGREDIENTS

- 1 cup butterhead lettuce
- 1 avocado, pitted and sliced
- 1/2 cup aioli
- 1 pound shrimp, peeled and deveined
- 1/2 cup cucumber, chopped
- 1 shallot, thinly sliced
- 1 tablespoon soy sauce
- 2 teaspoons fresh lemon juice

DIRECTIONS

1. Cook your shrimp in a pot of salted water for about 3 minutes. Drain and reserve.

2. In a salad bowl, mix all Ingredients, except for the lettuce leaves. Gently stir to combine.

3. Storing

4. Place the shrimp in airtight containers or Ziploc bags; keep in your refrigerator for up 3 to 4 days.

5. For freezing, arrange the cooked shrimp in a single layer on a baking tray; place in the freezer for about 15 minutes, or until it begins to harden.

6. Transfer the frozen shrimp to heavy-duty freezer bags. Freeze up to 3 months. Defrost in your refrigerator.

7. Place your salad in airtight containers or Ziploc bags; keep in your refrigerator for up 3 to 4 days. Mound the salad onto the lettuce leaves and top each portion with shrimp. Enjoy!

Cod Fish with Broccoli and Chutney

Preparation Time: 30 minutes Servings 4

NUTRITION: 291 Calories; 9.5g Fat; 3.5g Carbs; 42.5g Protein; 3g Fiber

INGREDIENTS

- 1 pound broccoli, cut into florets
- 1 teaspoon paprika
- 1 ½ pounds cod fish
- 2 Spanish peppers, thinly sliced
- 1 onion, thinly sliced
- 2 tablespoons sesame oil
- Sea salt and freshly ground black pepper, to taste

For Tomato Chutney:

- 1 cup tomatoes, chopped
- 1 teaspoon sesame oil
- 2 garlic cloves, sliced
- Sea salt and ground black pepper, to taste

DIRECTIONS

1. In a frying pan, heat 2 tablespoons of sesame oil over a moderately high flame.

2. Stir in the broccoli florets, Spanish peppers, and onion until they've softened; season with salt, black pepper, and paprika; reserve.

3. In the same pan, sear the fish for 4 to 5 minutes per side.

4. To make the chutney, heat 1 teaspoon of sesame oil in a frying pan over a moderately high heat. Sauté the garlic until just browned or about 1 minute.

5. Add in the chopped tomatoes and continue to cook, stirring periodically, until cooked through. Season with salt and pepper to taste.

6. Storing

7. Place the cod fillets with sautéed broccoli mixture in airtight containers and keep in your refrigerator for up to 3 to 4 days.

8. For freezing, place the cod fillets with sautéed broccoli mixture in airtight containers or wrap tightly with freezer wrap. Freeze up to 2 to 3 months.

9. Place the tomato chutney in airtight containers or Ziploc bags; keep in your refrigerator for up 3 to 4 days.

10. Defrost in the refrigerator and serve with the tomato chutney. Enjoy!

Classic Fish Tart

Preparation Time: 45 minutes Servings 6

NUTRITION: 416 Calories; 34.2g Fat; 5.5g Carbs; 19.5g Protein; 1.5g Fiber

INGREDIENTS

For the Crust:

- 1 teaspoon baking powder
- Flaky salt, to taste
- 1/2 stick butter
- 1 cup almond meal
- 3 tablespoons flaxseed meal
- 2 teaspoons ground psyllium husk powder
- 2 eggs
- 2 tablespoons almond milk

For the Filling:

- 10 ounces cod fish, chopped
- 2 eggs
- 1 teaspoon Mediterranean spice mix
- 1 ½ cups Colby cheese, shredded

- 1 teaspoon stone-ground mustard
- 1/2 cup cream cheese
- 1/2 cup mayonnaise

DIRECTIONS

11. Thoroughly combine all the crust Ingredients. Press the crust into a parchment-lined baking pan.
12. Bake the crust in the preheated oven at 365 degrees F for about 15 minutes.
13. In a mixing dish, combine the Ingredients for the filling. Spread the mixture over the pie crust and bake for a further 25 minutes.
14. Storing
15. Slice your tart into six pieces; divide between airtight containers or Ziploc bags; keep in your refrigerator for up to 3 days.
16. For freezing, place the pieces in airtight containers or heavy-duty freezer bags. Freeze up to 3 months. Once thawed in the refrigerator, heat in the microwave until warmed through. Enjoy!

Spicy Fish Curry

Preparation Time: 25 minutes Servings 6

NUTRITION: 270 Calories; 16.9g Fat; 5.6g Carbs; 22.3g Protein; 1.5g Fiber

INGREDIENTS

- 2 pounds pollock, cut into large pieces
- 1 teaspoon fresh garlic, minced
- Salt and black pepper, to taste
- 1 cup coconut milk
- 4 Roma tomatoes, pureed
- 2 tablespoons sesame oil
- 1 cup white onions, chopped
- 8 fresh curry leaves
- 2 tablespoons fresh lime juice
- 2 green chilies, minced
- 1/2 tablespoon fresh ginger, grated
- 1 teaspoon mustard seeds
- 1 tablespoon ground coriander

DIRECTIONS

1. Drizzle the fish with lime juice.
2. Heat the sesame oil in a frying pan over a moderately high flame. Cook the onion, curry leaves and garlic for 3 to 4 minutes until tender and aromatic.
3. Add in the ginger, salt, pepper, tomatoes, mustard seeds, and ground coriander. Let it simmer for 12 minutes or until thoroughly cooked.
4. Add in the fish and coconut milk and continue to cook, partially covered, for 6 to 7 minutes longer.
5. Storing
6. Spoon the fish curry into airtight containers; it will last for 3 to 4 days in the refrigerator.
7. For freezing, place the fish curry in airtight containers or heavy-duty freezer bags. Freeze up to 4 to 6 months. Defrost in the microwave or refrigerator. Bon appétit!

Crab Cakes

Preparation Time: 10 minutes Cooking Time: 15 minutes

Serve: 4

Ingredients:

- 1 egg
- 2 tbsp butter
- 1 tbsp cilantro, chopped
- 1/2 cup almond flour
- 4 tbsp pork rinds
- 1 lb crab meat
- 3 tsp ginger garlic paste
- 2 tsp sriracha
- 2 tsp lemon juice
- 1 tsp Dijon mustard
- 1/4 cup mayonnaise

Directions:

1. Add all ingredients except butter in a large bowl and mix until well combined.

2. Preheat the oven to 350 F.

3. Heat butter in a pan over medium- high heat.

4. Make crab cake from mixture and place in the pan and cook for 5 minutes.

5. Transfer pan in preheated oven and bake for 10 minutes.

6. Serve and enjoy.

Nutritional Value (Amount per Serving):

Calories 251

Fat 16 g

Carbohydrates 7.4 g

Sugar 0.9 g

Protein 15 g

Cholesterol 97 mg

Shrimp & Broccoli

Preparation Time: 10 minutes Cooking Time: 7 minutes

Serve: 2

Ingredients:

- 1/2 lb shrimp
- 1 tsp fresh lemon juice
- 2 tbsp butter
- 2 garlic cloves, minced
- 1 cup broccoli florets
- Salt

Directions:

- Melt butter in a pan over medium heat.
- Add garlic and broccoli to pan and cook for 3-4 minutes.
- Add shrimp and cook for 3-4 minutes.
- Add lemon juice and salt and stir well.
- Serve and enjoy.

Nutritional Value (Amount per Serving):

Calories 257

Fat 13 g

Carbohydrates 6 g

Sugar 0.9 g

Protein 27 g

Cholesterol 269 mg

Baked Salmon

Preparation Time: 10 minutes Cooking Time: 35 minutes

Serve: 4

Ingredients:

- 1 lb salmon fillet
- 4 tbsp parsley, chopped
- 1/4 cup mayonnaise
- 1/4 cup parmesan cheese, grated
- 2 garlic cloves, minced
- 2 tbsp butter

Directions:

1. Preheat the oven to 350 F.
2. Place salmon on greased baking tray.
3. Melt butter in a pan over medium heat.
4. Add garlic and sauté for minute.
5. Add remaining ingredient and stir to combined.
6. Spread pan mixture over salmon fillet.
7. Bake for 20-25 minutes.
8. Serve and enjoy.

Nutritional Value (Amount per Serving):

Calories 412

Fat 26 g

Carbohydrates 4.3 g

Sugar 1 g

Protein 34 g

Cholesterol 99 mg

Sour Cream Tilapia

Serves: 3

Prep Time: 3 hours 10 mins

Ingredients

- ¾ cup homemade chicken broth
- 1 pound tilapia fillets
- 1 cup sour cream
- Salt and black pepper, to taste
- 1 teaspoon cayenne pepper

Directions

1. Put tilapia fillets in the slow cooker along with rest of the ingredients.
2. Cover the lid and cook on low for about 3 hours.
3. Dish out and serve hot.

Nutrition Amount per serving

Calories 300

Total Fat 17.9g 23% Saturated Fat 10.7g 54%

Cholesterol 107mg 36%

Sodium 285mg 12%

Total Carbohydrate 3.9g 1% Dietary Fiber 0.2g 1%

Total Sugars 0.4g Protein 31.8g

Tilapia with Herbed Butter

Serves: 6

Prep Time: 35 mins

Ingredients

- 2 pounds tilapia fillets
- 12 garlic cloves, chopped finely
- 6 green broccoli, chopped
- 2 cups herbed butter
- Salt and black pepper, to taste

Directions

1. Season the tilapia fillets with salt and black pepper.
2. Put the seasoned tilapia along with all other ingredients in an Instant Pot and mix well.
3. Cover the lid and cook on High Pressure for about 25 minutes.
4. Dish out in a platter and serve hot.

Nutrition Amount per serving

Calories 281

Total Fat 10.4g 13% Saturated Fat 4.3g 21%

Cholesterol 109mg 36%

Sodium 178mg 8%

Total Carbohydrate 9g 3% Dietary Fiber 2.5g 9%

Total Sugars 1.9g

Protein 38.7g

Roasted Trout

Serves: 4

Prep Time: 45 mins

Ingredients

- ½ cup fresh lemon juice
- 1 pound trout fish fillets
- 4 tablespoons butter
- Salt and black pepper, to taste
- 1 teaspoon dried rosemary, crushed

Directions

1. Put ½ pound trout fillets in a dish and sprinkle with lemon juice and dried rosemary.
2. Season with salt and black pepper and transfer into a skillet.
3. Add butter and cook, covered on medium low heat for about 35 minutes.
4. Dish out the fillets in a platter and serve with a sauce.

Nutrition Amount per serving

Calories 349

Total Fat 28.2g 36% Saturated Fat 11.7g 58%

Cholesterol 31mg 10%

Sodium 88mg 4%

Total Carbohydrate 1.1g 0% Dietary Fiber 0.3g 1%

Total Sugars 0.9g Protein 23.3g

Sour Fish with Herbed Butter

Serves: 3

Prep Time: 45 mins

Ingredients

- 2 tablespoons herbed butter
- 3 cod fillets
- 1 tablespoon vinegar
- Salt and black pepper, to taste
- ½ tablespoon lemon pepper seasoning

Directions

1. Preheat the oven to 3750F and grease a baking tray.
2. Mix together cod fillets, vinegar, lemon pepper seasoning, salt and black pepper in a bowl.
3. Marinate for about 3 hours and then arrange on the baking tray.
4. Transfer into the oven and bake for about 30 minutes.
5. Remove from the oven and serve with herbed butter.

Nutrition Amount per serving

Calories 234

Total Fat 11.8g 15% Saturated Fat 2.4g 12%

Cholesterol 77mg 26%

Sodium 119mg   5%

Total Carbohydrate 0.4g 0% Dietary Fiber 0g 0%

Total Sugars 0.1g Protein 31.5g

Grilled Salmon

Preparation Time: 10 minutes Cooking Time: 25

minutes

Serve: 4

Ingredients:

- 4 salmon fillets
- 1 tsp dried rosemary
- 3 garlic cloves, minced
- 1/4 tsp pepper
- 1 tsp salt

Directions:

1. In a bowl, mix together rosemary, garlic, pepper, and salt.
2. Add salmon fillets in a bowl and coat well and let sit for 15 minutes.
3. Preheat the grill.
4. Place marinated salmon fillets on hot grill and cook for 10-12 minutes.
5. Serve and enjoy.

Nutritional Value (Amount per Serving):

Calories 240

Fat 11 g

Carbohydrates 1 g

Sugar 0 g

Protein 34 g

Cholesterol 78 mg

Salmon with Sauce

Preparation Time: 10 minutes Cooking Time: 3
minutes

Serve: 4

Ingredients:

- 1 lb salmon
- 1/2 lemon juice
- 1 tbsp garlic, minced
- 1 tbsp Dijon mustard
- 1 tbsp dill, chopped
- 1 tbsp mayonnaise
- 1/3 cup sour cream
- Pepper
- Salt

Directions:

1. Preheat the oven to 425 F.
2. In a bowl, mix together sour cream, lemon juice, dill, Dijon, and mayonnaise.
3. Place salmon on baking tray and top with garlic, pepper, and salt.
4. Pour half sour cream mixture over salmon.
5. Cover and bake for 20 minutes. Uncover and bake for 10 minutes more.

6. Serve with remaining sauce.

Nutritional Value (Amount per Serving):

Calories 213

Fat 12 g

Carbohydrates 3.1 g

Sugar 0.3 g

Protein 23 g

Cholesterol 59 mg

Salmon Patties

Preparation Time: 10 minutes Cooking Time: 10 minutes

Serve: 3

Ingredients:

- 14.5 oz can salmon
- 4 tbsp butter
- 1 avocado, diced
- 2 eggs, lightly beaten
- 1/2 cup almond flour
- 1/2 onion, minced
- Pepper
- Salt

Directions:

1. Add all ingredients except butter in a large mixing bowl and mix until well combined.
2. Make six patties from mixture. Set aside.
3. Melt butter in a pan over medium heat.
4. Place patties on pan and cook for 4-5 minutes on each side.
5. Serve and enjoy.

Nutritional Value (Amount per Serving):

Calories 619

Fat 49 g

Carbohydrates 11 g

Sugar 2 g

Protein 36 g

Cholesterol 225 mg

Tuna Salad

Preparation Time: 5 minutes Cooking Time: 5
minutes

Serve: 2

Ingredients:

- 5 oz can tuna, drained
- 1 tsp Dijon mustard
- 2 tbsp dill pickles, chopped
- 1 tbsp fresh chives, chopped
- 2 tbsp mayonnaise
- Pepper
- Salt

Directions:

1. Add all ingredients into the large bowl and mix well.

2. Serve and enjoy.

Nutritional Value (Amount per Serving):

Calories 143

Fat 5.6 g

Carbohydrates 4 g

Sugar 1 g

Protein 18 g

Cholesterol 25 mg

Flavors Shrimp Scampi

Preparation Time: 10 minutes Cooking Time: 25 minutes

Serve: 4

Ingredients:

- 1 lb shrimp, peeled and deveined
- 4 tbsp parmesan cheese, grated
- 1 cup chicken broth
- 1 tbsp garlic, minced
- 1/2 cup butter

Directions:

1. Preheat the oven to 350 F.
2. Melt butter in a saucepan over medium heat.
3. Add garlic and sauté for minute. Add broth and stir well.
4. Add shrimp to glass dish and pour butter mixture over shrimp.
5. Top with grated cheese and bake for 10-12 minutes.
6. Serve and enjoy.

Nutritional Value (Amount per Serving):

Calories 388

Fat 27 g

Carbohydrates 2.7 g

Sugar 0.2 g

Protein 30.4 g

Cholesterol 307 mg

CPSIA information can be obtained
at www.ICGtesting.com
Printed in the USA
LVHW022100020221
678130LV00004B/502